Dance!
To Improve Riding and Driving Your Horse

BROUGHT TO YOU BY

The books created by Equine Heritage Institute are designed to preserve the history and majesty of the horse. Our goal is to find, understand, and pass on the valuable data about equine use and its influence on humanity. The Equine Heritage Institute is a not for profit 503(c) and 100% of all proceeds from the sale of books, services, and products support Equine Heritage Institute's mission.

To make a donation to EHI, please visit www.ehi-donations.com

SPECIAL THANKS TO OUR TEAM

Mary Chris Foxworthy, Research Writer

Mary Chris Foxworthy's grandfather owned one of the last creameries in the United States that still used horse-drawn milk wagons; thus began a life-long love affair with horses. After graduating from college with a degree in Food Science and Communications, Mary Chris bought her first horse with her first paycheck. After graduation she worked in Marketing and Finance in the corporate world. During that time, she volunteered her Marketing and Fundraising skills for various non-profits and finally in 2006 left the corporate world to work in the area of Advancement until her retirement in 2016. She has served on the board of various equine associations and held a judge's card in Carriage Driving. She has published and presented numerous equine educational programs, written for several equine publications and won an award from American Horse Publications for one of her articles. Mary Chris is an active exhibitor in Carriage Driving and Dressage. Along with her husband, she enjoys spending time with their horses (three Morgans and a PRE), a bouncing Bearded Collie and two adult children."

Abby David, Graphic Designer

Abby David's family has roots in the Walking Horse tradition and she grew up hearing tales of Ole Tobe the mule's antics, holiday wagon decorations, and trick riding. In her teens she spent her summers boarding the neighbors horses and playing at barrel racing in the back paddock with Thunder. She landed a job as a Graphic Designer at The Arts Center of Cannon County in 2004 and has worked in the print and digital mass communications industry continuously. Since marrying into a family in the racehorse business, David Racing Stables and Ortiz Racing Stables, she has enjoyed exploring a whole new world of horses and wearing big fancy hats. She also enjoys dancing in all it's forms and teaches in her local community.

Gloria Austin's Collection of Books

www.GloriaAustin.com

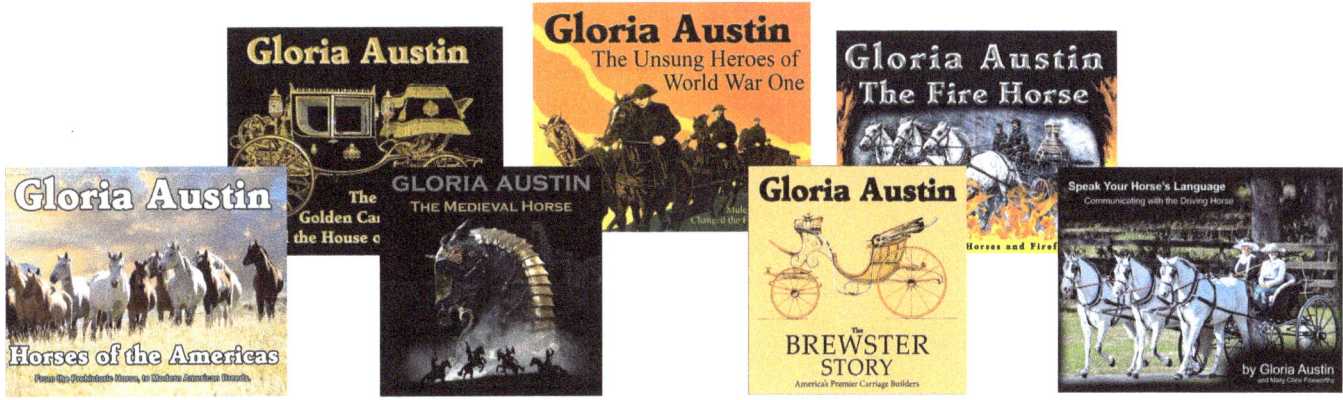

ENJOY OUR OTHER BOOKS

- How a Horse Can Make You a Better Dancer
- The Brewster Story
- Carriage Lamps
- Gloria Austin's Carriage Collection
- A Glossary of Harness Parts
- Equine Elegance
- The Fire Horse
- Horse Basics 101
- The Unsung Heros of World War One
- The Horse, History, and Human Culture
- Horses of the Americas
- A Drive Through Time: Carriages, Horses, and History
- Speak Your Horse's Language
- Tea: Steeped in Tradition
- The Golden Carriage and the House of Hapsburg
- The Medieval Horse
- Concord Coach - Staging and Freighting
- Coaches and Coaching Throughout the Ages
- Horse Symbolism

Brought To You By The Equine Heritage Institute

Dance! To Improve Riding and Driving Your Horse
By: Gloria Austin President of Equine Heritage Institute, Inc. (EHI)
and Mary Chris Foxworthy

First Publish Date 2019
Copyright © 2019 by Equine Heritage Institute, Inc.

All rights reserved. No part of this publication may be reproduced, distributed, or transmitted in any form or by any means, including photocopying, recording, or other electronic or mechanical methods, without the prior written permission of the publisher, except in the case of brief quotations embodied in critical reviews and certain other noncommercial uses permitted by copyright law. For permission requests, write to the publisher, addressed "Attention: Permissions Coordinator," at the address below.

Gloria Austin Carriage Collection, LLC; Equine Heritage Institute, Inc.
3024 Marion County Road Weirsdale, FL 32195 Office: (352) 753-2826 Fax: (352) 753-6186

Ordering Information:
Quantity sales: Special discounts are available on quantity purchases by corporations, associations, and others. For details, contact the publisher at the address above.
Printed in the United States of America
Print - 978-1-7339860-9-0, Ebook - 978-0-692-13979-0

Table of Contents

INTRODUCTION..9
RHYTHM AND TEMPO..10
    Understanding Music..11
    Rhythm - The Horse...13
Rhythm - Dancing...14
    Tempo - The Horse..17
Tempo - Dancing..21
    Rhythm and Tempo Wrap-up..22
STAMINA and FITNESS..23
    The Fitness of the Horse..24
    Stamina and Aerobic Fitness for You...25
MUSCLE STRENGTH AND FLEXIBILTY...29
    Muscle Strength and Flexibility: Riding and Driving...................................30
    Core Muscles...31
    Developing core muscles by dancing!..32
    DANCE YOUR WAY TO SUCCESS: Core Muscles..................................35
    Upper Back, Neck, Shoulders and Arms..42
    Let's develop upper body strength by dancing!..43
    DANCE YOUR WAY TO SUCCESS: Upper Body Muscles.......................46
    Quadriceps and Hamstrings...51
    Let's develop lower body strength by dancing!..52
    DANCE YOUR WAY TO SUCCESS: Lower Body Muscles......................55
VISUALIZATION...60
Physical and Mental Visualization..61
    Dancing with Your Eyes...62
    Dancing in Your Mind's Eye...64
    DANCE YOUR WAY TO SUCCESS: Visualization...................................66
INTENTION..73
    Planning with Intention...74
    Communicating with Intention..75
PARTNERSHIP..79
    Magical Partnerships...80
    Creating the Magic..81
APPENDIX - STEPS IN BUILDING A FIT HORSE..90
SOURCES..94

The Horse

"We have had 6,000 years of history with the domesticated horse and only 100 years with the automobile."
Gloria Austin

INTRODUCTION

Have you tried Yoga, Zumba or Pilates all in an effort to improve your riding? As an equestrian, you know that any combination of these just scratches the surface of the skills necessary to ride or drive a horse.

There is a form of exercise that can give you all the skills needed to become a fit and good rider or driver; it's fun and something you can do with a partner or a group which makes it even more enjoyable. This form of exercise is dancing! Ballroom dancing, tap, jazz, hip-hop and even line dancing are a few of the many types of dancing that will help to improve your riding and driving.

Most people who do not ride find it hard to believe that riding or driving a horse is the ultimate mental and physical exercise. It's a difficult concept to explain to others, especially when they think the horse is doing all the work. To be a good rider or driver you need stamina. You need balance. You need core strength. You need a sense of rhythm. You need concentration. You need to form a partnership with a thousand-pound animal and so much more! Let's find out why!

RHYTHM AND TEMPO

Understanding Music

Music is its own language; one just like you would read aloud from a book. All of the symbols and writing on a sheet of music represent the pitch, speed, and rhythm of the song as well as the expression and techniques used by a musician to play the piece. That sounds like riding a horse, right?

We are the "sheet music". We have to let the horse know what we want with our aids – legs, seat, hands and voice. Our aids are like the symbols on a page of sheet music. Our aids need to tell the horse what tempo and rhythm we want and many more things. You need to understand rhythm and tempo for dancing too so that your steps and body movements can flow with the music.

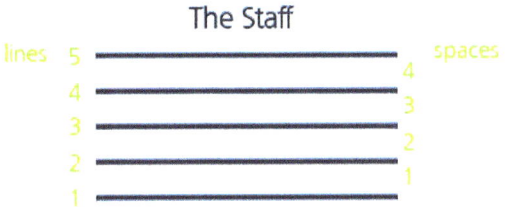

Music is written on a staff and the lines and spaces on a staff indicate what note is to be played.

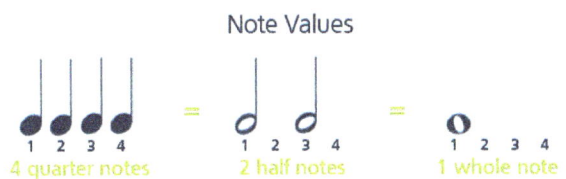

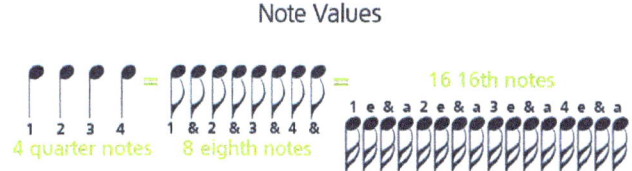

Each note written on the staff has a value, and the way a note is drawn tells you what the value is for that note.

In order to play music, you need to know its meter. Meter is the arrangement of rhythms in a repetitive pattern; it is the beat you use when clapping or tapping your foot along with a song. When reading music, the meter is presented similar to a fraction, with a top number and a bottom number; we call this the song's time signature. The top number tells you how many beats to a measure. The bottom number tells you the note value for a single beat. A measure is the space of staff in between each vertical line, and the beat is the pulse your foot taps along with while listening. In the example below, the time signature is 4/4, meaning there are 4 beats per bar and that every quarter note gets one beat.

Horses have a rhythm too. Horses have "gaits". The typical gaits of a horse are walk, trot, canter and gallop. Each gait of a horse has a defined rhythm. Rhythm is important for dancing too. Dancing is a fixed sequence of basic steps with a defined time signature.

In addition to your note values and time signature, the last piece to feeling the rhythm is knowing your tempo or beats per minute. Tempo tells you how fast or slow a piece is intended to be played. Words at the top of the page of music tell the musician how fast to play the music. A tool called a metronome can be set to make a ticking type of noise for the number of beats per minute that you want. If you are going to play music, ride a horse or dance, you should get a metronome. You can even get a simple metronome app for your phone. (cited from: https://www.musicnotes.com/blog/2014/04/11/how-to-read-sheet-music/)

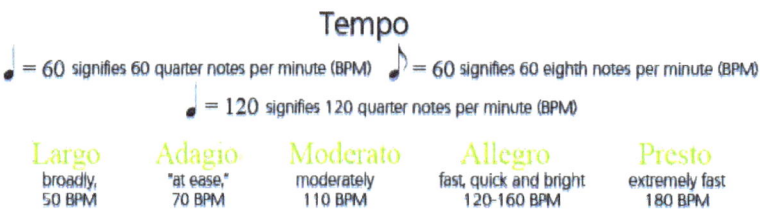

Rhythm - The Horse

The basic gaits of a horse are walk, trot, canter, and gallop. Each of these gaits has a rhythm. The rhythm of these gaits does not change; even if the speed (tempo) changes, the rhythm stays the same.

The walk is a four-beat gait.

The trot is a two-beat gait.

The canter is a three-beat gait.

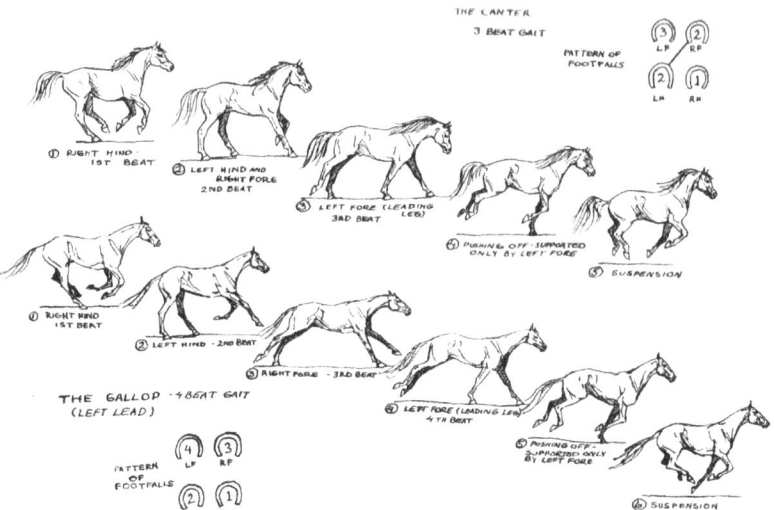

The gallop is a four-brat gait.

Rhythm - Dancing

A good sense of rhythm is important in dance. Remember that meter is the arrangement of rhythms in a repetitive pattern and shown as a fraction on the musical staff. The upper number shows how many beats are in a measure, and the lower number shows which note gets one count.

Ballroom Dancing

In Ballroom Dancing, the various dances have very specific rhythms. For example, the Rumba is 4/4 time, the Waltz is in 3/4 time, and the Tango is in 2/4 time. The steps of the dance are either "quick" or "slow". "Slow" steps take twice as many beats as "quick" steps. For example, in the Rumba, the music is written in 4/4 time but all step patterns have 6 steps completed in 8 beats or 2 measures. The dance time will be " slow, quick, quick, slow, quick, quick". The slow step takes 2 beats and the quickstep takes 1 beat.

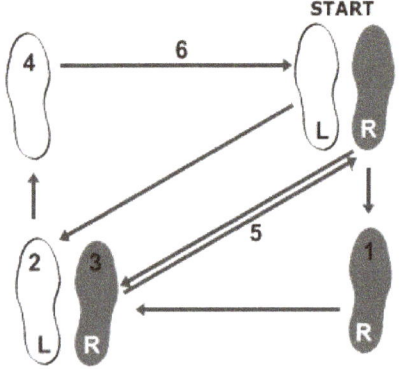

Rumba

1. Step back with your right foot
2. Sidestep to the left with your left foot
3. Move your right foot to your left foot
4. Step forward with your left foot
5. Sidestep to the right with your right foot
6. Move your left foot to your right foot

Tap Dancing

Tap dance is a type of dance characterized by using the sounds of tap shoes striking the floor as a form of percussion. That means that rhythm is very important in tap dancing since you can closely hear when the dancer is not in rhythm with the music. Tap dancers use syncopation too. That means that they interrupt the rhythm with an offbeat step but, if timed incorrectly, it can sound very bad.

Ballet

Ballet is a selection of steps, rhythms, and so much more! Ballet is not just rhythmic gymnastics on pointe; meaning the position where the body is balanced on the tip of the toe. Ballet is very interpretive and thus a rhythmical sense and musicality are crucial when dancing. It is an interpretation of the music within the rhythm of the music.

Have you ever seen the Nutcracker Ballet? If you have seen different versions of it, you have probably seen different interpretations. It's the same music while the selection of steps may be different, yet the rhythm of the music is still followed by the chosen steps. The Cecchetti Method of teaching ballet emphasizes the importance of training the dancer's ear to distinguish the rhythm of the music so that the dancer's movements are in strict harmony with the measure.

Tempo - The Horse

Within the rhythm of each gait, the tempo SHOULD remain the same. If the horse goes from a free walk to a medium walk, the tempo should remain the same. If the horse goes from a medium trot to a lengthen trot, the tempo should remain the same. This is not easy; the horse needs to be well schooled and well-muscled to maintain tempo. The rider also needs to have a good sense of the rhythm and tempo in order to regulate the tempo.

Medium trot

Lengthen trot

Find Your Horse's Tempo

One of the best ways for a rider to learn how to regulate the tempo is to ride with music. To do this you will need a metronome. (right) There are several free metronome apps that you can download and some that you can pay for that have advanced features.

Have someone make a video of you riding your horse at each gait; you will need about 5 minutes at each gait. While watching the video, use the metronome to decide how many BPM (beats per minute) the horse has at each gait.

- For the walk, count the front legs only. The normal BPM at the walk will be 104 BPM to 112 BPM.
- For the trot, count each beat; remember it will be a 2 beat. The trot will normally fall between 135 BPM and 165 BPM.
- For the canter, count the strike of the leading foreleg. The BPM for the canter normally falls between 93 BPM and 105 BPM.
- For both the walk and trot you can divide the BPM in half and songs with those BPMs will also work (52 BPM to 56 BPM for the walk and 67 BPM to 82 BPM for the trot).
- Using the slower BPM for a horse that has quick, choppy strides can fool the eye and make the horse seem smoother.

Now, search for songs at the noted BPMs for each of your horse's gaits. Play the songs while watching the videos you made until you find several songs that are a good match. Download these songs to a listening device and ride to them.

Riding to music is relaxing and fun. You will find that you soon learn to regulate the tempo of each gait. Some horses even seem to be more responsive when you ride to THEIR music!

More About the Trot

The trot is a two-beat diagonal gait. It is important to be on the correct diagonal to help develop the rhythm. When referring to "being on the correct diagonal", we are speaking about the rider, not the horse. Riders will often "post" at the trot too. Posting is when a rider rises out of his or her seat for every other stride of the horses' forelegs. Why? Posting helps a horse to develop their rhythm.

You will often hear an instructor say, "rise and fall with the leg on the wall". If you are not riding indoors there will, of course, be no wall so wall means the "outside" or convex side of the horse; when a horse travels in a circle he will have a convex side and a concave side. To be on the correct diagonal, the rider will rise when the outside front leg is forward and the inside hind foot is on the ground. When the horse changes direction, the rider changes their posting diagonal. If the rider does not change their posting diagonal, the horse could lose its balance or rhythm.

There is another good reason for posting besides helping the horse to maintain rhythm. Sitting when the inside hind leg is on the ground allows the rider to ask the horse for more engagement while his inside hind leg is still on the ground. Without your weight on the next step as you rise, the horse's inside hind leg can move more freely as it leaves the ground. As the inside hind leg swings more under the body and becomes stronger it improves the horse's self-carriage, allowing the forehand to lighten and the horse to become free in the shoulders. (cited from: https://dressagetoday.com/theory/purpose-posting-trot-outside-diagonal-heather-mason)

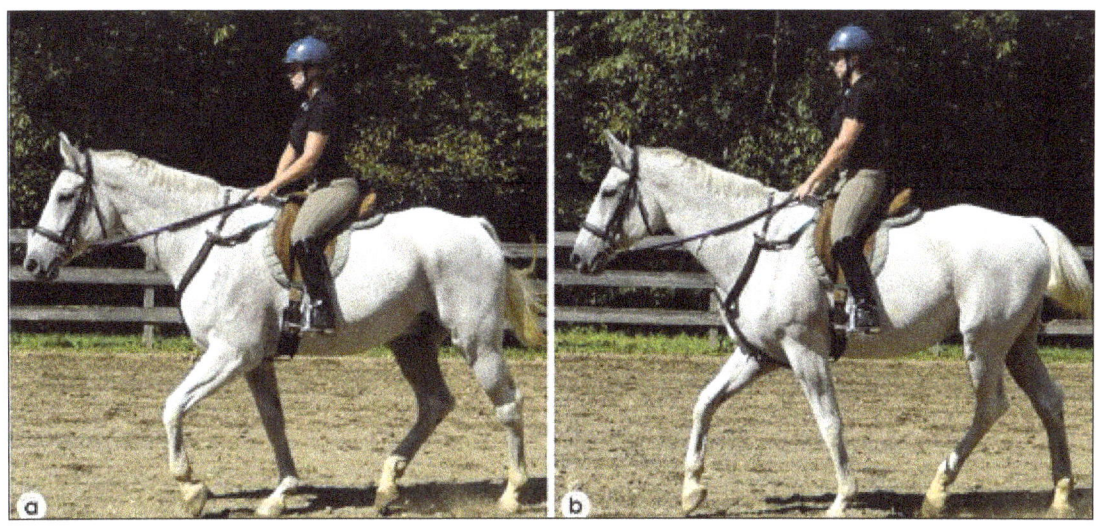

a) sitting with inside hind leg   b) rising with outside front leg

Fun Fact!

Why is it called "posting"?

Hundreds of years ago the nobles traveled in carriages. They did not want non-nobles in the carriages driving with them, so they had postillion riders, who rode on the near horse of a pair and guided both horses from the saddle. Most of the horses they used for their carriages were high-stepping horses with lots of bounce. This made it rather uncomfortable for the "post boys", as they were called, to sit the trot. They discovered that if they came out of the saddle every other stride that it was much more comfortable – hence "posting".

Tempo - Dancing

Understanding how tempo relates to rhythm, for dancing, helps with learning how to understand rhythm and tempo with horses.

The rhythm of a dance does not change – the Rumba is " slow, quick, quick, slow, quick, quick". The slow step takes 2 beats and the quickstep takes 1 beat. The rhythm of a horse's gait will also not change; the walk will always be 4 beats, the trot 2 beats and the canter 3 beats.

Each type of dance in Ballroom Dancing has a suggested range of BPMs for that dance. Just like the gaits of a horse generally fall within a range of BPMs, dances have specific BPMs. For example, the suggested BPM for the Rumba is 104-144. The suggested BPM for a trot is 135-165.
A "shuffle ball change" in Tap Dancing is a 4-beat movement, the speed of the movement will change with the tempo of the music but, the rhythm will not change. For horses it is a little different. The rhythm of the gait stays the same and, for a well-schooled and well-muscled horse, the tempo should remain the same within the gait.

In ballet, the "pas de cheval" has a syncopated rhythm (slow, quick), no matter the tempo of the music that rhythm does not change but the tempo of the music may change the speed of the movement. By the way, "pas de cheval" means "horse step" and it is a step that mimics the pawing of a horse. A good sense of tempo in relation to rhythm is important in dance. It is very important that steps are taken on the correct beat (rhythm) and at the correct speed for the music (tempo). For dancing, the tempo of the beat will change with the music so a dancer needs to learn to make the rhythm work with the tempo. For equestrians it's a little different. The rhythm of a gait always stays the same and the rider or driver needs to learn to keep the tempo of the gait the same within the rhythm – this is VERY difficult!

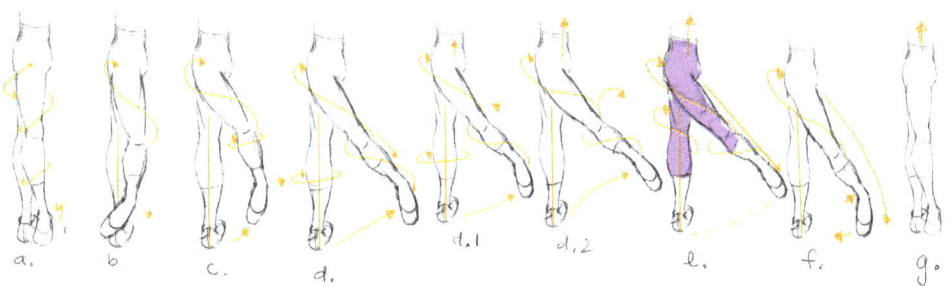

How to perform a **pas de cheval**

Rhythm and Tempo Wrap-up

An easy way to understand the relationship of rhythm and tempo is to think of driving a car over rumble strips. When you drive over the strips you hear a rhythm. The rhythm of the rumble strips is the same no matter how many times you drive over them. This is because the distance between the strips does not change. However, depending on the speed you travel the tempo of that rhythm will change.

Music has rhythm and tempo. Dancing interprets the rhythm and tempo of the music. Horses have rhythms and tempos influenced by the skill of the rider or driver.

Having a sense of rhythm and tempo is extremely beneficial when riding and driving horses, and it's easy to see how any kind of dancing can help to develop these skills.

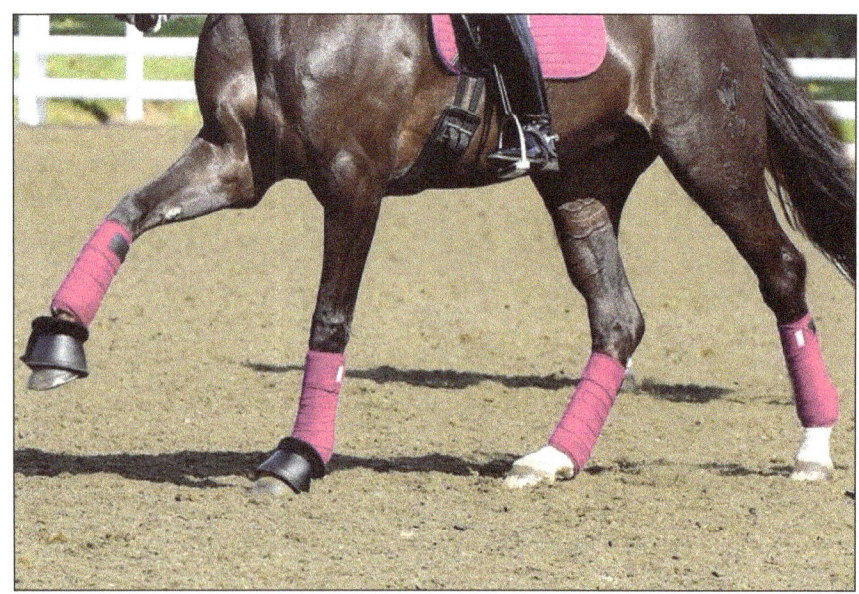

STAMINA AND FITNESS

The Fitness of the Horse

Before we proceed with getting YOU in shape to ride or drive a horse, it is important to make sure the horse is fit too! You would not go out and run a marathon without training and getting in shape and the same goes for your horse. Your horse needs to be in shape for any activity to prevent any injuries and perform well. Fitness is not just determined by the muscular and skeletal fitness of the horse, but also by the attention, willingness, coordination, and energy level of the horse. Below is a quick review of the steps involved in getting a horse fit.

Steps in Building a Fit Horse

There are 3 phases to building a horse that is fit.

1. Preparation phase
   Building the top line
   Increasing attention, willingness and coordination
2. Cardio Phase – measuring and increasing fitness
   Building the energy level/stamina
   Improving recovery time
3. Strength building (schooling) - the muscular and skeletal building blocks of fitness. It is best to work with your trainer to develop a strength building exercise program for the specific discipline of the horse which will include:
   Exercises to improve muscular and skeletal integrity
   Exercises to improve abilities

(refer to "Steps in Building a Fit Horse" in the appendix at the back of the book for more information)

Stamina and Aerobic Fitness for You

Equine related activities burn calories and increase strength, flexibility, and stamina.

There is no doubt that equestrians and horse owners need to stay in shape. Driving, riding, and caring for a horse requires a lot of hard work. An equestrian needs good stamina and aerobic fitness. Through many daily activities, people are able to burn lots of calories, and many of those activities require the equestrian to be in good shape. The chart below gives you an idea of how many calories are burned during common activities.

ACTIVITY:	For 130 lb person:	For 155 lb person:	For 190 lb person:
Shoveling	354 cal/hr	422 cal/hr	518 cal/hr
General Horse Riding:	236 cal/hr	281 cal/hr	345 cal/hr
Riding horse at the walk:	148 cal/hr	176 cal/hr	216 cal/hr
Riding horse at the trot:	384 cal/hr	457 cal/hr	561 cal/hr
Riding horse at a gallop:	472 cal/hr	563 cal/hr	690 cal/hr
Horse Grooming	354 cal/hr	422 cal/hr	518 cal/hr
Baling hay/cleaning barn:	472 cal/hr	563 cal/hr	690 cal/hr
Shoveling Grain	325 cal/hr	387 cal/hr	474 cal/hr
Fencing	354 cal/hr	422 cal/hr	518 cal/hr
Polo	472 cal/hr	563 cal/hr	690 cal/hr
Hiking, cross country (if your horse is hard to catch...)	354 cal/hr	422 cal/hr	518 cal/hr
Brisk walking 4 MPH	236 cal/hr	281 cal/hr	345 cal/hr
Walking, carrying 15 lb load:	207 cal/hr	246 cal/hr	302 cal/hr

What is Aerobic Fitness?

Stamina comes from aerobic fitness and is the ability to sustain work for prolonged periods. It enables you to ride without gasping for breath, and to drive your horse cross-country without tiring. "Cardio" work - which gets your heart pumping for at least 20 to 30 minutes at a time - is also needed to develop this sort of endurance.

During sustained exercise, your muscles depend on oxygen to metabolize carbohydrates and fats into energy. Your heart pumps that oxygenated blood to your muscles. When your heart cannot keep up with the muscles' demand for oxygen, you experience fatigue. Aerobic exercise is what gets your heart fit so that it can keep up with the demand to pump oxygenated blood to your muscles. You should participate in an aerobic exercise about 3 times a week. Each aerobic workout needs to get your heart pumping for at least 20 to 30 minutes at a time. It is important to monitor your heart rate in order to improve your endurance and fitness.

To do this, you need to monitor the BPM (beats per minute) of your heart just like monitoring the horse's BPM while analyzing its gait. There are many fitness devices and apps to help you do this. It is recommended that you exercise within the 50 to 85 percentiles of your MHR (maximum heart rate) for at least 20 to 30 minutes to get the best results from aerobic exercise. See the table below to determine your heart rate.

Age	Maximum HR	50 percent	75 percent	85 percent
20	200	100	150	170
25	195	98	146	166
30	190	95	142	161
35	185	93	138	157
40	180	90	135	153
45	175	88	131	149
50	170	85	127	144
55	165	83	123	140
60	160	80	120	136
65	155	78	116	132
70	150	75	113	127
75	145	72	108	123
80	140	70	104	119
85	135	68	101	115

What exercises are aerobic exercises?

Varying the type of exercise you engage in is important. Doing so tunes your muscles to different movements and different intensities helping you achieve overall fitness and athleticism. Swimming, jogging, skating, cross-country skiing, and cycling are all forms of aerobic exercise. You can also do aerobic exercises at home. A typical 30-minute workout is outlined in the chart on the left.

Many forms of aerobic exercise are exercises or activities that you do by yourself. On the other hand, exercising with a friend has many benefits. The friend helps to keep you motivated, makes the time go by faster and most of all makes it way more fun!

Dancing is aerobic exercise...and it's fun!

Dancing offers a great workout for the cardiovascular system as it requires a large degree of flexible movement. According to the Mayo Clinic website, dance can count toward your 90-minute per week aerobic exercise goal. Dancing is a whole-body workout that's fun at the same time. Most forms of dance keep you moving for long lengths of time while simultaneously bringing oxygen to your heart and elevating its rate.

Have you ever gone line dancing with a group of friends? Dancing is so much fun that you may forget you are exercising at the same time! The workout you get from dancing depends on the type of dance you do and how long you do it for. For example, ballroom dancing will give you a moderate workout. This is about the same level of exercise you would get from walking briskly or doing water aerobics. More intense types of dance, such as tap dancing, will give you a more vigorous workout that is similar to jogging or swimming laps. You can burn up to 500 calories an hour with this type of dance. On the other hand, ab crunches only burn about 168 calories and are not nearly as much fun. (cited from: https://medlineplus.gov/ency/patientinstructions/000809.htm and https://woman.thenest.com/dance-aerobic-anaerobic-15312.html)

MUSCLE STRENGTH AND FLEXIBILITY

Muscle Strength and Flexibility: Riding and Driving

Muscle strength enables you to use the various parts of your body effectively to cue and control your horse. Of special interest are your core muscles found in your midsection. This includes your abdominals, lower back, and inner thighs. A strong core makes everything you do, including riding and driving, easier. It also enhances balance and protects your back from injury. Strong arms and legs are also key to the effectiveness of a rider or driver. Exercises and movements that target key muscle groups will develop this muscle strength.

Flexibility is the ability of your muscles and joints to achieve a full range of motion. As a rider or driver, you need flexibility in order to follow your horse's motion (to "be with" your horse) and to remain relaxed and secure in the saddle or on the box seat. (cited from: https://www.equisearch.com/articles/exercise_better_ride_021110)

Regular exercising of all major muscle groups is key to good muscle strength and flexibility. Even just sitting in the correct position requires muscle control, strength, and flexibility. Unlike running, cycling, or other forms of exercise, dancing doesn't always repeat the same motion over and over again, so it's perfect for strengthening the many muscles needed for riding and driving. Dancing requires isolating body parts and trains your body to be symmetrical and synchronized – exactly what is needed for riding and driving a horse! To understand more about the importance of good muscle strength and flexibility, you need to know more about each key muscle group.

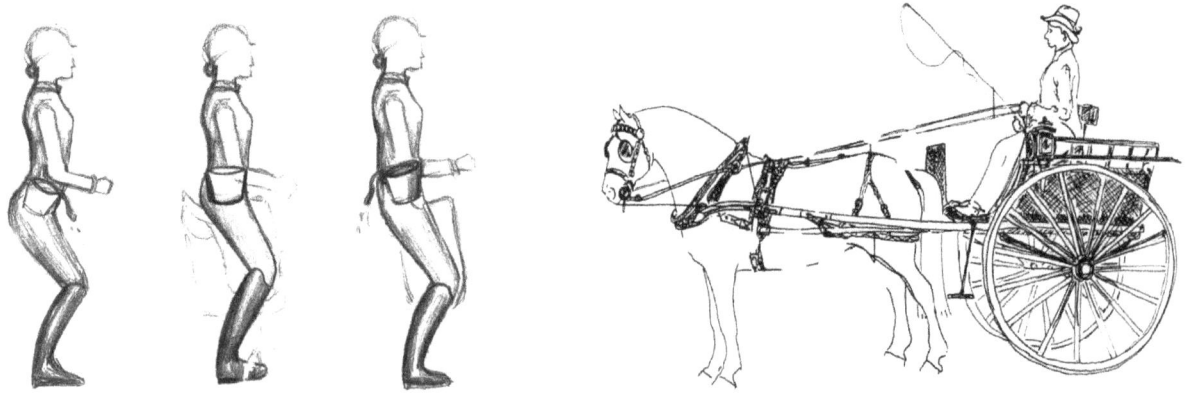

Core Muscles

The muscles in your abdomen are known as your "core". Strong abdominal muscles support the upper and lower back and help to maintain seat and balance. Weak abdominal muscles contribute to poor balance and contribute to lower back pain. It is important to keep the lower back loose to avoid such pain. Lower back muscles work continuously to stabilize your upper body and absorb natural concussions. Upper back muscles aid posture and help to support muscle balance for the lower back. The core muscles are the foundation of the human body. All of the muscles in your body at some point rely on your abs, hips, and lower back.

The core refers to any muscle that attaches to the spinal column or the pelvis, which means that back pain can come from an imbalance or injury to any of these muscle groups.

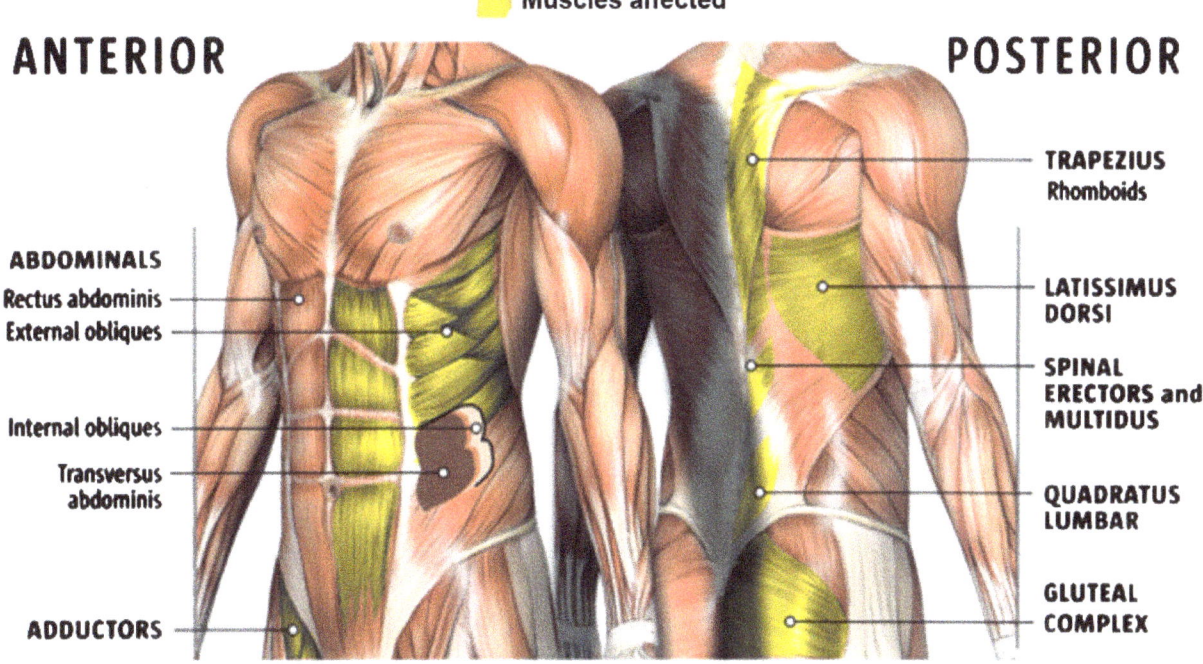

Developing core muscles by dancing!

Dancing is one of the best ways to help develop strong core muscles. No matter the style, dancing is a workout!

Ballroom Dancing

In ballroom dancing, maintaining a proper partnering frame engages the core. The frame is an important element used by both partners to create the upper body shape and help hold the partner with elevated arms and an open chest. A strong core is used to create and maintain a strong frame. The male partner needs to know where the female dancer's center is at all times. Both partners need to hold their waists firm to provide stability at the pelvis for quick footwork and challenging movements. Without a strong core, you won't have good posture and won't be able to create powerful forward or backward movements since the frame depends on the core to hold steady, all while dancing.

Tap Dancing

In tap dancing, the dancers must hold the spine firm throughout all of their combinations. Their torso placement must be intensely secure so they can move their legs and feet with incredible speed. Tap dancing teaches you how to balance, and because weight shifts, it is a great way to enhance your balance and core control. In tap dancing, the dancers move in all directions which is excellent for balance. Tap dancing connects the feet with core control. It also requires the body to balance, shift, and quickly adjust itself over fast-moving feet. The feet create the "music" but the entire body creates the dance.

You can tap dance at home by yourself; the quick-paced music often associated with tap dancing is a great motivator! You can tap dance with a group too. Clogging, Irish step dancing, and even some line dancing all have similar benefits to building core strength.

Ballet

Classical ballet gives the illusion of being lifted, light, and of airy quality. The foundation of ballet stems from five basic positions with the legs turned out. These positions require strict centering and abdominal control. A strong core is extremely important for placement, turns, jumps, landing, and pointe work. Ballet engages the core in every step. Even in the most basic steps, ballet dancers are pulling in to maintain that beautiful posture.

During a jump, the first thing a ballet dancer does is breathe in using the diaphragm, which activates the core. Then, the dancer uses her abs and glutes to prep for the jump, perform the jump, and support her body when she lands so that she can do so softly. Ballet dancers practice movements adagio – that means very slowly. The dancers use slow, sustained movements like lifting one leg and turning. This super-slow movement forces their cores to keep readjusting to accommodate their movements. Just learning the 5 basic positions of ballet is a great start to strengthening your core! (cited from: https://delta.dance/2018/09/training-muscles-for-ballroom-dance, /https://www.quickquickslow.com/blog/how-ballroom-and-latin-dancing-build-core-strength, http://www.humankinetics.com/excerpts/excerpts/role-of-the-core-in-dance-techniques, https://www.womenshealthmag.com/fitness/a19928590/ballerina-core-tips/)

DANCE YOUR WAY TO SUCCESS: Core Muscles

Imagine: You need to lengthen your horse's frame and gait.

You need to loosen your lower back in order to use your seat to move the horse forward, out, and down.

Dance Your Way to Success
The combination of a plié and squat with a leg lift will help you understand the feeling of loosening your back while using your seat. So, turn on "Swan Lake" and dance like a ballerina!

CORE MUSCLES

Imagine: You are sitting the trot/jog.

You need to keep your lower back loose in order to move with the horse.

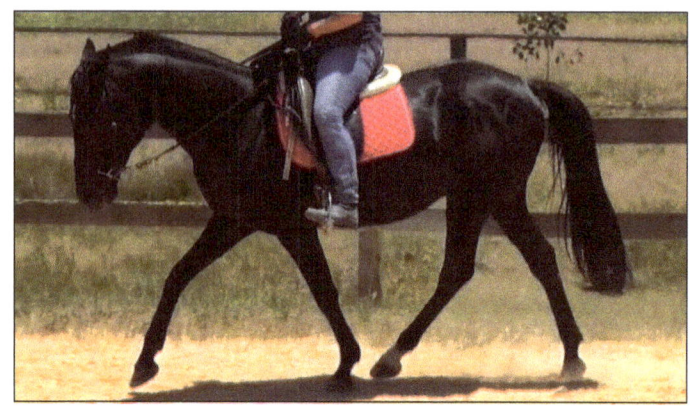

Dance your way to success

Latin style dancing is a great way to loosen the lower back. The hip movements in these dances require flexibility in the hips while the core remains still.

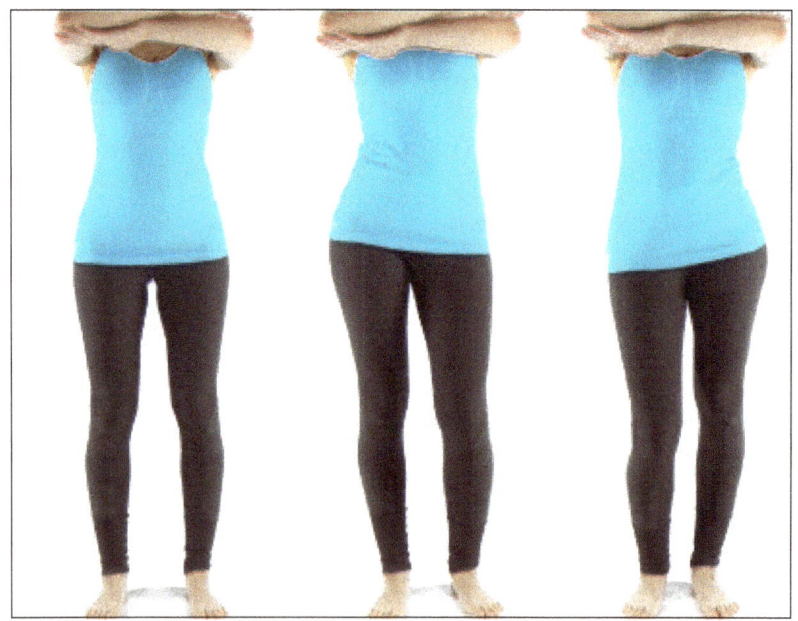

CORE MUSCLES

Imagine: You are cantering/loping and bouncing out of rhythm with your horse.

You need to: loosen your lower back to absorb the concussion between you and the saddle and move with your horse.

Dance your way to success

A great move in hip hop dancing is the chest-pop followed by the pelvic tilt. This is a great dance move to help learn how to isolate your seat and core in order to absorb and move with the horse.

CORE MUSCLES

Imagine: Your horse has lost his tempo and he is speeding up.

You need to activate your core to give your horse a half halt cue with your seat.

Dance your way to success

Belly dancing is another wonderful way to learn how to activate your core. The popular "figure 8" move will help to strengthen the core while keeping hips flexible.

CORE MUSCLES

Imagine: Your horse has become tense because you have tightened your legs or hands.

You need to relax your legs and hands and, using your core, quiet your seat to be in rhythm with your horse and control his tempo.

Dance your way to success
Many ballet moves are great for your core and so much more. In this case, practicing an arabesque with extension will help to strengthen the core while keeping arms and hands soft.

CORE MUSCLES

Imagine: You are riding a tough course!

You need to engage your core muscles to stay with the motion of your horse through jumps, turns and cross country sprints in order to avoid fatigue.

Dance your way to success

Gather up your friends and head out clogging or, if near St. Patrick's Day, try some Irish step dancing. Both types of dance are not only great for building stamina but really work the core for an extended length of time. Plus, it's fun to dance with friends!

Imagine: You are making a circle with your horse, and he is pushing into your inside leg so that you can't bend him.

You need to use your core to center yourself so that your horse can't push you to the outside.

Dance your way to success
Hip hop dancing can help to activate the core while keeping hips flexible. Turn up your favorite jam, and move your legs and arms to the beat!

CORE MUSCLES

Upper Back, Neck, Shoulders and Arms

The back anatomy includes some of the most massive and functionally important muscles in the human body. Your upper back helps to stabilize your lower back and aids in posture. The back muscles also enable you to reach, pull, and extend your arms. The latissimus dorsi, also known as the "lats" or "wings," is the largest and most well-known of all the back muscles. Your lats help you in pulling and reaching with your arms and support your body in a variety of movements and situations. The teres major muscles are located underneath the lats. They work in conjunction with the rotator cuff muscles. This group of muscles aid in pulling the arms downwards and rotating them inwards. The trapezius muscles are located between your shoulders and your neck. They control the shoulder blades which play a role in shrugging, neck movement, and head support. The rhomboid muscle is located on the upper portion of the back anatomy, underneath the trapezius. The rhomboid muscle is activated as you bring and squeeze your scapula or shoulder blades back and together.

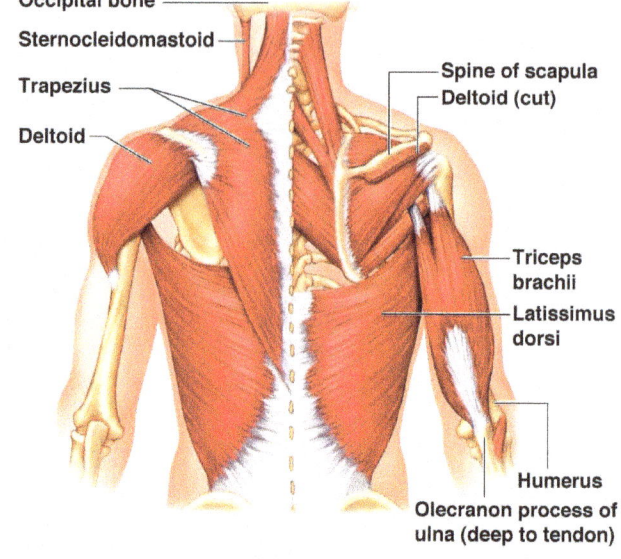

It is important to keep your upper back connected to shoulders, arms and lower back and to keep your neck relaxed. Keeping your neck relaxed helps to prevent tension and keeps your eyes focused ahead. All of this is very important when you ride or drive a horse. (cited from: https://www.kingofthegym.com/back-anatomy/)

Let's develop upper body strength by dancing!

Ballroom Dancing

Good posture and stretching are very important for ballroom dancers. The upper back, neck, and shoulder muscles are critical for maintaining the posture and flexibility required to dance. The "lats" are used to keep arms in position when they are raised up; it helps your arms from becoming fatigued when held in positions for an extended period of time. When these muscles are strong, you can hold your arms level with less effort or fatigue, and you can keep your shoulders from rising up or hunching forward. In Latin dancing, the lats are engaged as the dancer extends their arms. The action begins in the back and then extends to the elbow and finally to the hand. It's similar to how you throw a Frisbee. (cited from: https://delta.dance/2018/09/training-muscles-for-ballroom-dance/)

Tap Dancing

Tap dancing is very fluid and involves quick movements. Tap dancers and jazz dancers have to isolate body parts in order to emphasize the music. A turn cannot successfully be completed with droopy elbows. Jumps will not get far off the ground if shoulders and neck are tensed. To achieve proper turns, jumps and other movements, it is important to move the arms from the center of the back—not from the shoulders. Fluid arms and polished hands finish the picture that fast-flying feet begin in tap dancing. When the arms are fully integrated, they make a tap routine a dance rather than an exercise. When a tap dancer is not controlled up top, they lose clarity, strength, and speed in their feet. If the arms or the head are drooping, it weighs the dancer down. The arms need to counter the legs in a gentle swing in order to introduce the upper body into footwork. "Street tap" helps the arms to become loose. Tap dancing can help to relieve tension in the upper back, neck, and shoulders because it is a form of dance where the dancer "feels the groove" and moves with it. (cited from https://www.dance-teacher.com/armed-for-tap-2392320922.html)

Ballet

You may have heard the term épaulement when people speak of great ballerinas. What is Épaulement? In French épaulement (ay-Pohl-MAHN) means "shouldering." In ballet, it refers to the position of the shoulders, head, and neck. When a ballerina is praised for her "good épaulement," it means she has combined lovely upper-body work and artistic expression seamlessly. As ballet dancers move through positions, they need to coordinate the head, arms, legs, and shoulders. The ability to do this comes from the upper back, rather than lifting from the shoulders, which will cause tension in the body. (cited from https://www.dancespirit.com/the_importance_of_ epaulement-2326036463.html)

DANCE YOUR WAY TO SUCCESS: Upper Body Muscles

Imagine: You want to check the bend or straightness of your horse.

You need to look straight ahead, not down, and feel the position of your horse through the position of your upper body, through your seat.

Dance your way to success

Have you ever wondered how figure skaters spin so fast without getting dizzy? They use the same technique that dancers use called "spotting". When Ballroom dancers twirl or ballerinas do a pirouette, they "spot" which is to fix their gaze on a single location. Learning to "spot" while dancing will help you to maintain position on your horse while looking straight ahead.

Imagine: Your horse sees something unusual and now your horse is distracted and so are you.

You need to keep you and your horse focused. Keeping your shoulders square without dipping to one side or drooping; use your upper body and turn your horse towards the "spooky" item.

Dance your way to success
So many forms of dancing require stabilizing the torso and then isolating it from the hips. Have fun with some Latin dancing or ballet dancing and even line dancing to help develop a secure upper body and an independent seat.

UPPER BODY MUSCLES

Imagine: Your horse bolts and jumps to the side.

You need to keep your upper back loose, relaxed, and connected to your lower back. Allow your seat to follow the movement of the horse.

Dance your way to success

Belly dancing is another dance form that helps to develop a flexible yet connected torso. Just add the finger cymbals and you have a complete work out for your upper body!

UPPER BODY MUSCLES

Imagine: You are on a cross country drive and your arms are becoming fatigued.

You need to relax your shoulders and engage your "lats" to support your arms.

Dance your way to success
When dancing, hold props like ropes or canes to keep arms positioned properly. This will increase the muscle strength needed to hold your arms in position while riding and driving.

UPPER BODY MUSCLES

Imagine: Your horse is frightened, and the first thing you do is lean forward in survival mode and grab the reins.

You need to relax by dropping or rolling your shoulders and look up; this helps to stop you from leaning forward. Then, loosen your arms and wiggle your fingers like you are squeezing a sponge.

Dance your way to success

Ballet will help to create soft yet effective hands and arms. In ballet, it is important that hands and arms are delicate. However, do not confuse delicacy with weakness! The idea is for the arms to look graceful but feel strong. Try this at the barre: With the working arm held to the side, look "over" by slightly lifting the head up and to the right over the arm, then look "under" by slightly inclining the head down and to the right, as if looking under the arm.

UPPER BODY MUSCLES

Quadriceps and Hamstrings

The quadricep muscles are a group of muscles on the front of your thighs. There are four distinct muscles that make up the quadricep muscles; hence the name "quads". The four quad muscles have individual names and are located in different positions on the front of each of your thighs.

All four quadriceps are powerful extensors of the knee joint. If you sit in a chair and straighten your knee a few times, you can see and feel the quads in action on the front part of your thigh. When your quads contract, they straighten your leg at your knee joint. They are crucial in walking, running, jumping and squatting. The rectus femoris muscle is a flexor of the hip. It has two heads; the straight head has its origin on the anterior inferior iliac spine and the reflected head has its origin on the ilium. This flexor action is also crucial to walking or running as it swings the leg forward into the ensuing step. The quadriceps, specifically the vastus medialis, play the important role of stabilizing the patella and the knee joint during gait.

The hamstrings are a group of muscles and their tendons at the rear of the upper leg. You use the hamstrings for walking, running and jumping. They flex the knee and extend the hip at the beginning of each step. In walking and running, they are antagonists to the quadricep muscles in the action of deceleration of knee extension. Because the hamstrings have their origin at the sitting bones, they are extended while sitting and long periods of sitting may affect their function. (cited from: https://www.verywellhealth.com/ , https://en.wikipedia.org/wiki/Quadriceps_femoris_muscle)

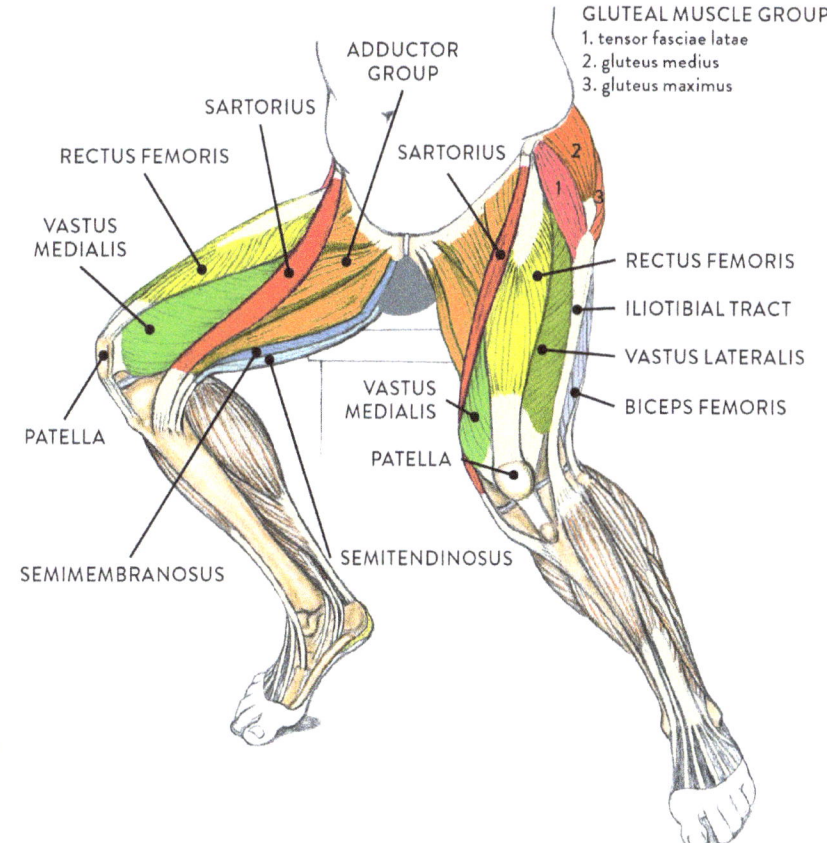

Let's develop lower body strength by dancing!

Ballroom Dancing

If you do a movement, such as a man's *Contra Check*, in Ballroom dancing and hold it for a long time you will feel the quads and hamstrings in action! The man turns his body left face, flexes his knees, and steps forward on his left foot with strong contra-body action. Contra-body action occurs when one steps with one foot (in this case, the left) but leads with the opposite side of the torso (in this case, the right). As he steps forward, he turns his left toe out for greater stability. Many of the leg and hip movements in Ballroom dancing call on the quads and hamstrings!

Tap Dancing

The majority of the actions that a tap dancer performs originate at the knee and hips. A back brush of the toe doesn't come from depressing the ankle down, but by swinging the whole section of the leg, backwards, under the knee. The first scraping sound of a wing isn't produced by the foot scraping the toe, but by a loose ankle rolling over from the outward force originating from the hip. The rule for the knee in tap dance is to get it over the toes.

Providing that the ankles are left loose and relaxed, your heels will lift up almost magically. When the heel is then pressed to the floor and released, the heel will pop back up thanks to the natural elasticity of your body. Strong hamstrings and quads help to achieve this.

Have you ever seen the famous Radio City Music Hall Rockettes? Rockette Tara Dunleavy, a Radio City Rockette, explains that, "… we have to master those eye-high kicks that we are famous for and what many people don't realize is that we don't touch each other's backs when we are linked up in the kick line. So not only do our legs have to be strong enough to do that many kicks, but our core needs to be working extra hard to be able to maintain our spacing and stay in a straight line." (cited from:https://www.danceadvantage.net/steal-from-ballet-for-tap/, https://www.health.com/fitness/rockettes-leg-exercises)

Ballet

Ballet dancers use their hamstring muscles in order to straighten their leg as they lift it to the front or to the side, while strong quadriceps are needed to be able to get one's leg up to about 90 degrees. Ballet dancers appreciate the aesthetic quality of a straight leg line, so they work hard to consistently achieve long and high leg extensions.

As a result, dancers typically develop strong quadriceps, the muscles that assist with full knee extension and hip flexion. At the same time, dancers understand the functional advantage of deep knee bends. The *plié*, or kneebend, is a fundamental move in ballet, and every time a dancer bends her knees into plié, her hamstrings cotract. Consequently, a dancer's hamstrings become increasingly strong and powerful as she progresses in her training. (cited from: https://www.livestrong.com/article/548392-what-muscles-does-dancing-ballet-strengthen/)

DANCE YOUR WAY TO SUCESS: Lower Body Muscles

Imagine: Your horse is speeding up at the trot.

You need to support him to keep him under himself. Do this by slowing your post to control his tempo.

Dance your way to success
Hip-Hop is fast and fun. Try doing a front, side, back kick to strengthen the quads and hamstrings.

LOWER BODY MUSCLES

Imagine: Your horse is not moving forward consistently.

You need to check *how* you are posting. Make sure you are not pushing upwards using hands, upper body swing, or relying on stirrups as if they were a springing platform.

Dance your way to success
While practicing ballet, try a second position plié to help strengthen your quads while learning to rely on them for the lift rather than the feet.

LOWER BODY MUSCLES

Imagine: You are launching out of the saddle at the rising trot.

That's a good thing! That means the horse is doing the work to lift you at the trot. You should not push yourself out of the saddle at the rise phase. Now just use your hamstrings to pull yourself back into the saddle

Dance your way to success
The Grand Batement and Rond de Jambe are both great ballet movements for working quads and hamstrings.

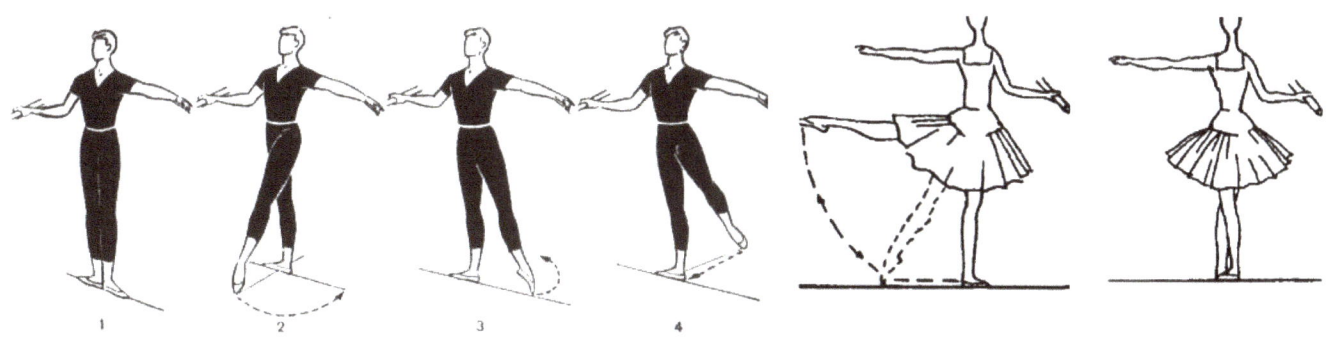

Rond de Jambe   Grand Batement

LOWER BODY MUSCLES

Imagine: Your leg has swung too far forward.

You need to use your hamstring muscles to pull your leg back and keep it under you.

Dance your way to success

Dance like a Rockette! Those high kicks they are famous for are perfect for strengthening hamstrings.

LOWER BODY MUSCLES

Imagine: You are having a hard time keeping your leg quiet.

You need to let your hamstring bend your knee. This allows you to stabilize your seat so that your leg is quiet.

Dance your way to success
The dance moves "Rodeo Kick" and "Figure 4" (named for the way the body looks like a 4!) in line dancing are great dance moves to learn how to use your hamstring and knee together.

LOWER BODY MUSCLES

VISUALIZATION

Physical and Mental Visualization

When you were younger your parents at some point probably said, "watch where you're going!" They said this to keep you safe. You learn to use your vision, your eyes, to "watch where you're going". The same is true in riding and driving your horse; you need to focus on where you want to go. In dancing, you don't watch your feet, you watch where you are going. This is physical visualization.

Have you ever seen a shirt or a pair of pants and thought, "that would look good on me!" When we ride or drive a horse, we have a visual image of how we want to look, just like imagining what it would be like to wear that shirt or pair of pants. When we dance we also have a visual image of how that dance should be performed. This is *mental visualization*.

Unlike other forms of exercise, dancing requires lots of visualization, both physical and mental, in order to perform the required steps and movements. Visualization is imperative for riding and driving horses too.

Josie Walsh -Photo by Jody Q. Kasch

Dancing with Your Eyes

Most dance studios are lined with mirrors, and many dancers feel mirrors help them to visualize their alignment. When absorbing choreography, dancers often observe their instructor while physically practicing behind them. Dancers learn by watching! Watching in order to learn is important but at some point, the dancer needs to develop confidence. In studios dancers often get in the habit of looking into the mirrors or watching the instructor instead of looking in the direction of the movement. Likewise, looking down at the feet is not following the direction of the movement. The eyes should always be pointing in the same direction as the nose.

One of the most crucial things in partner dancing is eye contact. Eye contact is a tool that helps you connect and communicate with your partner without speaking. Looking at your partner and observing their body language can provide a tremendous amount of important information. If you don't look at your partner, you will risk missing out on a lot of leads and cues, thus making it very difficult to dance together. The Latin and rhythm dances such as salsa, cha-cha, mambo, swing, and hustle require a lot of eye contact since you are usually facing your partner while dancing with them.

The leader also needs to be watching the entire dance floor so that he does not lead his partner into another couple! For certain moves, dancers want to be looking straight ahead, or slightly away from their partner, in order to keep their shoulders and torso in the correct alignment. Many times, it is crucial to look in the direction of the movement; this is especially important for the leader in executing turns. However, the partner doesn't need to look at the leader during the spin or turn. In fact, the partner should look at their own hand if possible and use it as a reference point to spot the spin or turn.

We have already mentioned epaulement in relation to combining lovely upper-body work and artistic expression in ballet. Epaulement is characterized by the harmonious shapes made by the relationship between the torso and head as well as the direction of the eyes. In ballet, some believe that using the eyes to "direct" the dance makes the difference between the technically strong and the technically beautiful. Competitive dancers know that making eye contact (and maintaining eye contact) with the judges or the audience exudes a special confidence that allows them to be seen as capable and talented performers. It's not a staring contest though; it's an invitation that says, "look at me, watch what I can do!"(cited from: https://salsabortropical.com/eye-contact-and-sense-of-touch-when-you-are-dancing/, http://www.danceaustralia.com.au/news/the-importance-of-eyeline1, https://www.dancespirit.com/do-this-not-that-how-to-be-the-master-of-eye-contact-2473329173.html, https://hubpages.com/entertainment/Where-to-Look-While-Partner-Dancing-The-Importance-of-Eye-Contact)

Dancing in Your Mind's Eye

Visualization is the act of using mental imagery to simulate your desired outcome in a given situation. Visualization goes beyond thinking positively about the desired outcome. During visualization exercises, you are focusing on your execution as you want it to be; in a way that's as true-to-life as possible. Science has proven that dancers can improve their technique, memorization, and performance by implementing regular visualization. What's really cool about visualization is that you don't need to have a dance studio in your home. Visualization doesn't require very much space at all. Dance is considered by many to be the ultimate "proving ground" for visualization. Many athletes use visualization to hone in on their skills – and many athletes also dance for that very reason – it helps to develop visualization skills! Hall of Famers Lynn Swann and Herschel Walker both took ballet classes as did Arnold Schwarzenegger and Jean Claude van Damme.

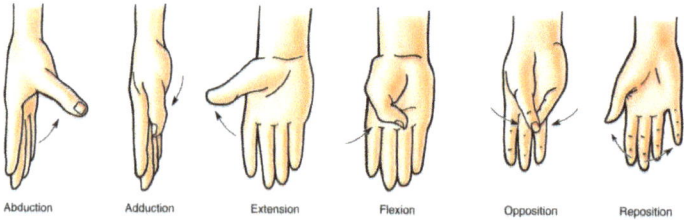

Our mind doesn't know the difference between what we really do and what we imagine. In a research test called *Little Finger Abduction*, a group performed visualization exercises with their hands and fingers. Overall, the group increased their finger abduction by 35%, while another group, who did not do any type of visualization exercises, did not improve at all. "If you can convince your mind that you can, your body has a better chance of following suit," says Vito Bernasconi, junior soloist of the Queensland Ballet.

Josie Walsh, an artistic director of the Joffrey Ballet School LA, says that, when choreographing, she has her dancers take a "visualization break". Everyone lies on the floor with their eyes closed. They visualize all the changes and corrections while the music is playing. Then, they get up and dance. "The results are huge!" Walsh exclaims. "Often times, we get caught in physical limitations and get stuck there, but visualization shows you a different route and then it's achievable. Also, it allows the space to focus on the nuances and bring that into the physical. Visualization and physicality together are the ultimate synergy." (cited from: https://www.danceinforma.com/2016/11/07/creativity-and-chaos-nederlands-dans-theater-director-paul-lightfoot/)

Visualization can help the dancer become so familiar with the dance that it settles the nerves and brings out the best in them. The dancer directs their mind to visualize the desired outcome; there is no fear and no self-doubt in the visualization. In the mind's eye, the dancer executes the movements perfectly. The trick is to make the visualization the reality. But it all starts with visualizing oneself doing the desired action perfectly. If you can't picture yourself doing it correctly, then how are you going to do it?

As equestrians, visualization, both physical and mental, are crucial to success. Start dancing! It will help you to develop visualization skills!

DANCE YOUR WAY TO SUCCESS: Visualization

Imagine: You are driving your horse through a cones course and you think you just knocked over a ball on cone #6.

You need to keep your eyes focused on the next set of cones. Don't look down! Looking down will turn your torso and go through your shoulders to your hands, adversely affecting the signal to your horse towards the next set of cones.

Dance your way to success
Dancing with a partner will help you learn to make and hold eye contact.

Imagine: You are entering the dressage ring for your test and the judge salutes. You return the salute and look down as you do.

You need to tip your head slightly while maintaining eye contact with the judge. Don't look down! Be sure to wear a confident smile when you do. This way you are focused the entire time on where you will be going next, and you communicate to the judge that you are confident and here to show him/her your best effort.

Dance your way to success
Dance in front of a mirror to practice visualization, eye contact, and self-confidence!

VISUALIZATION

Imagine: You are walking a cones course or jumping course and you are trying to determine the best route.

You need to not just walk the course in order to memorize it. You need to walk the course using the same angles, directions, strides and turns that you will take with your horse.

Dance your way to success
Much like walking a course, when you dance, you should look at yourself from the outside in to see your dancing exactly as you want it to be. Pay attention to your lines and extension and your movements in between your movements. You can pick different details to focus on in each session, but give yourself a purpose. Sometimes that means turning the music off and just focusing on how your foot brushes the floor.

Imagine You are at a new venue that you and your horse have never been to before. You are worried that your horse will spook at the unusual things near the ring.

You need to stay calm and focused. If you worry, your horse will too. Don't focus on the "stuff". Focus on looking ahead to where you are going. Then visualize how the ride or drive will go – completely forgetting about the scenery.

Dance your way to success
When you dance you want to create a complete picture; like where on the dance floor you will perform each move. You should build your mental environment as thoroughly and as close to reality as possible. If you're envisioning practice, make sure your mental venue looks like your physical one. Find a place to practice that will have distractions to practice staying focused.

VISUALIZATION

Imagine: Your horse always stands still at home, but in the line up at the show, he always fidgets.

You need to stop psyching yourself out that it's the show that makes bad things happen. It's you visualizing that bad things happen at a show! Instead, only visualize every step involved in doing it correctly all of the time.

Dance your way to success

Make your practice time, in your mind, as close to reality as possible. When a dance combination is giving you trouble, visualize it going perfectly while playing the music you will dance to. It takes a lot of practice in the studio for the Rockettes to get their famous synchronization.

VISUALIZATION

Imagine: You didn't win, and all you can think about is everything that you _think_ went wrong.

You need to think about your ultimate goals. Is just winning all that you wanted? Or did you just want the canter to be better? Remember what you were working on and be happy if you achieved that. Don't dwell on what went wrong. Especially during the ride! It just means you have something to work on for the next time.

Dance your way to success
When you dance in front of an audience the only one who knows if something went wrong is you. Remember, "the show must go on"! Visualize the next move and do it. The more you dance, the more you will gain confidence and learn to keep dancing no matter what happens.

VISUALIZATION

Imagine: You arrived late at the show and wanted to work on a few more things before your class - but that's not going to happen now.

You need to stay calm. Don't panic! At this point one more practice ride really is not going to make a big difference. Go to the show arena and calm yourself. Visualize your ride - picture in your mind, what you are going to wear and how amazing your horse will look after you groom him. Then, while enjoying grooming your horse, visualize your ride again with him near you.

Dance your way to success

Pick a time and a place, every day, where you can relax, close your eyes, and work through dance routines. The more you learn how to do this the more it will come in handy when you really need it!

VISUALIZATION

INTENTION

Planning with Intention

Observe this picture of a horse, rider, and dancer. What do you think is their intention? Do you think they had a plan for this performance? Can you imagine what could go wrong if they did not?

Choreography is the art or practice of designing sequences of movements of physical bodies in which motion, form or both are specified. Choreography is used for ice- skating, cheerleading, synchronized swimming, and even in designing freestyles for dressage. The intent of a choreographer is to make the audience obtain a certain emotion, feeling, or thought through the movements. The intent of the choreographer is very important!

Having intention means to go after your desires with a focus and purpose, not sitting idly wishing things would change. When you dance with intention, you are dancing with a focus and a purpose.

Communicating with Intention

Ballroom dancing with a partner is enjoyable – as long as you are not stepping on each other's feet! Dancing with a partner should never involve force or pressure. Ballroom dancing is about communicating - silently!

Intention is the action of the leader to the follower and the follower can, and should, respond. Leaders propose to their partners that they would like "X" to happen. Once the follower feels the intent to move, they should go and not wait to be pushed to do something..

A leader can apply force to the follower to get them to do what they want. This however, says that the leader must control the follower. It also says to the follower that the leader doesn't trust them and can't rely on them to listen to what they are telling them to execute. It also says that the follower will never, ever be able to hear the level of precision desired by the leader.

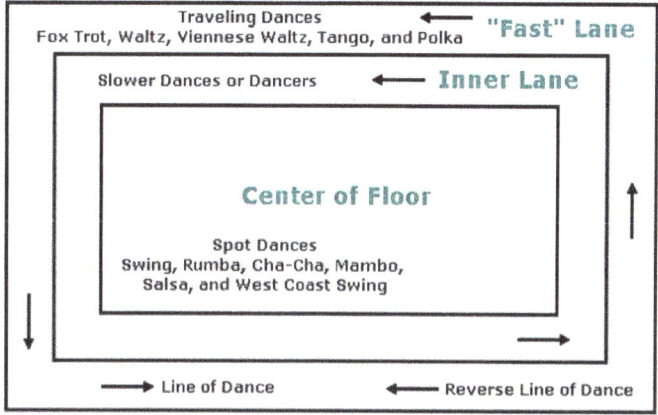

Ballroom dancers may be dancing with just one partner, but they share the floor with many other couples. When there are multiple dancers on the floor, it is important to know dance floor etiquette. This means that you and your partner must be aware and alert of your surroundings and keep communication clear between one another. Again – dancing with intention - knowing where you are supposed to be and where you are going.

Now let's put this in terms of riding or driving a horse. Asking a horse to achieve a movement should not involve force. When you ask the horse to do something, have you adequately prepared the horse for the movement? Is he balanced? Did you give a half halt to get his attention and let him know that you are about to ask for something? Was your cue accurate and timed well? If you are constantly nagging the horse or if you are inconsistent with your cues, the horse will not trust you. Most of the time the horse is only doing what you ask; they are the followers and we are the leaders. When it goes wrong, ask yourself first, what did I do? Don't blame the horse!

Often times you will be riding or driving with groups of horses and people. Like Ballroom dancing, there is etiquette to riding with a group. Usually in an arena, if going in opposite directions, it is always left shoulder to left shoulder. Faster horses have the outside. Like dancing, you need to have a clear intention with where you are going as well as with what you are attempting to achieve.

Imagine a tap dancer tapping with great speed and exuberance, completely out of tempo with slow music. The intention of the dancer is not in keeping with the intention of the music. Dance must be choreographed with the music in order to convey the intent. Let's use the example of the Nutcracker Ballet again. Can you imagine the Russian dancers doing their dance to the music of the Sugar Plum Fairy?

Dancers who are part of a troupe need to understand the intent of the choreographer, and they also need to learn to work together. They need to all have the same intent. It never looks good when one dancer is doing something different than the rest. Even in line dancing, everyone needs to be doing the same steps or there will be collisions.

It's important for dancers to be confident and have a positive attitude. They need to feel confident in what they are doing and in what they are thinking as well. It's okay to ask questions of the instructor or choreographer, but it's important not to overthink. People tend to dance better when they are not in their heads too much.

Let's relate this to working with horses. Some riders tend to over analyze every movement and become quite mechanical when they ask the horse for a particular movement. All horses are different and what works for one may not work for another. The cue for a shoulder-in is the same but how you apply the cue may be different on each horse. For example, the rider has an intention but they are not listening to the response they are getting from the horse so, the rider continues to ask the horse in the same mechanical way. The horse does not "answer the question" (do as asked by the rider) and the rider becomes frustrated. At this point, it's important to "ask the question" in a different way or to move on to something the horse understands; then go back to the movement that is not going as intended. Remember, most of the time it is the rider's or driver's fault that things are not going as intended

Some riders and drivers have a tendency to ignore their trainer (the choreographer). They think to themselves, "that IS what I am doing." However, obviously, it is not or the trainer would not be asking you to do it. The rider/driver needs to refocus and communicate with the horse via the watchful eyes of the trainer.

Dancing with groups and a choreographer or instructor can help equestrians learn how to communicate with their horse and trainer.

PARTNERSHIP

Magical Partnerships

The ideal dance partnership involves years of practice and togetherness as well as trust, empathy, and the ability to instinctively react in the moment. A successful dance partnership can never be taken for granted and is focused greatly on growth and success. It involves personal investment and emotion, like a life partnership. It also requires you to play your role, while assisting and compensating for each other when needed. Sounds like working with horses right?

The Nicholas Brothers

Margot Fonteyn and Rudolf Nureyev

Fred Astaire and Ginger Rogers

PARTNERSHIP

Creating the Magic

The following steps to a successful partnership, taken from "Dance Comp Review", really show how much a dance partnership can help to develop a partnership with your horse.

Never take your dance parter for granted. Since your partner is 50% of your success, you really need to make sure that you invest in each other in addition to taking care of your own needs.

Never take your horse for granted. Make sure he is happy and in good physical condition.

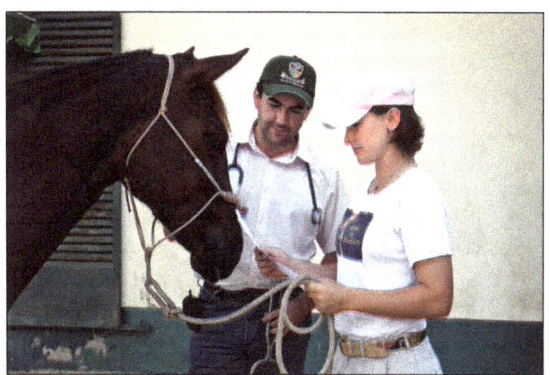

PARTNERSHIP

If your dance partner feels demoralized, not valued or fearful, their energy and focus will be on those feelings, and not on dancing. Make your partner feel like they are very special to you and you are grateful for what they do to make your partnership work.

If you are not in a good mood, do not take it out on your horse. If the horse misunderstands what you want, find another way to ask.

PARTNERSHIP

Dance partners should not avoid disagreements. They are sometimes necessary to move forward. It is also important not to hold back on opinions that are important to you just to avoid an argument. Arguments are only really harmful when they stop being about different opinions, and start being about wanting your partner to become a different person.

There will be set backs and that's OK. It's not OK to get mad at your horse though. Stay positive and think it through. When you try to figure out how to help your horse to be the best he can be, you become a better rider or driver.

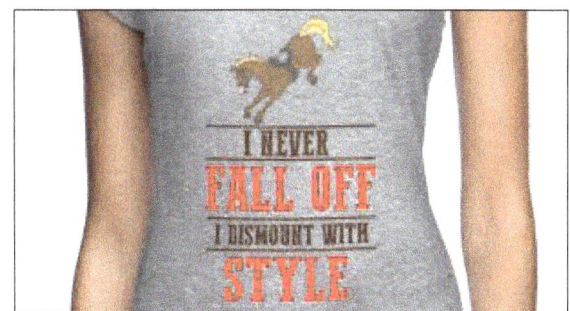

PARTNERSHIP

Each dance partner has skills, experience and passion that may be similar, but is almost always a bit different. Any difference is an amazing opportunity for couples to look to each other as additional teachers. Your partnership can get stronger and better very quickly when you seek the information and ideas of the other to support your own learning.

Riding or driving many different horses can help to develop more skills. Each horse is different and will present challenges that help the rider or driver to learn more.

PARTNERSHIP

Think of dance couples that are memorable and magical. To get to this level, there needs to be a lot of communication to find a common approach between partners, and a feeling of safety to experiment as a couple. If you shut each other down too quickly, the potential of being a memorable couple will never happen.

Trust your horse. To do this you must convey a positive attitude and help him to get through what is difficult for him. If he spooks at the tree or doesn't want to go through water, forget about it; if you dwell on it, he will pick up on it and just spook again! Instead, help him to forget about it with your positive attitude.

PARTNERSHIP

Lack of connection in partner dancing is unpleasant to watch, so the attention goes to even small weakness. Many things are important, but a big thing is whether you understand and are responding to the feeling and energy of your partner.

Learn your horse's signals that will tell you ahead of time that he needs a little extra inside leg to get through the corner. Sometimes just watching your horse's ears will tell you everything you need to know! If you are constantly communicating and picking up on the signals your horse gives you, you become a partnership that is fun to watch!

PARTNERSHIP

Goals are important to keeping dancers from becoming stagnant. Achieving small goals is very satisfying and can keep your motivation to stay together. Talking honestly early in the partnership about goals and the way to achieve them, will help and will prevent heartache later.

Set your goals and keep them realistic for both you and your horse. Be willing to make adjustments to the goals when either of you experience a set-back. Riders do not need to constantly be looking for a new horse to achieve a goal; horses can be lifelong partners. Maybe it's the goals that need to be adjusted for that horse or for the rider. Enjoying horses can be a lifelong pursuit!

PARTNERSHIP

So....start dancing to improve your riding, your driving and most of all your partnership with your horse!

You have half our gifts. I the other half. Together we make a whole. Together we are much more powerful. - Joss Stirling

APPENDIX

Steps in Building a Fit Horse

PREPARATION PHASE
- » Building the Top line: Back and Hindquarter Strengthening and Relaxing
- » Increasing Attention-Willingness-Coordination: Mind & Body Awareness

EXERCISE 1 (In Hand)
- » Set out a bale of hay or straw.
- » Walk the horse over the bale – encourage the horse to lift each leg rhythmically over the bale.
- » Once this is mastered, have the horse go as slowly as possible – especially hesitating the back legs as he goes over the bale.
- » Once this is mastered, set out several bales several feet apart and repeat.

EXERCISE 2 (In Hand)
- » Mark a 10-meter circle with cones.
- » Stand in front of your horse and slowly back your horse one step at a time around the circle.
- » Praise him often.
- » Do it in the opposite direction.

EXERCISE 3 (Can be done long lining or ridden)
- » Using the entire arena, slow trot on the short ends, and working trot on the long sides.
- » Transitions need to be smooth!

EXERCISE 4 (Can be done long lining or ridden)
- » Make a 20-meter circle at one end at a slow trot.
- » Coming out of the circle, go to the rail and trot once around maintaining tempo – do not allow the horse to speed up
- » Return to 20-meter circle maintaining tempo.
- » Repeat in the opposite direction.

EXERCISE 5 (Can be done long lining or ridden)
- » Set out 4 ground poles approximately 2.5 feet apart.
- » On a loose rein walk horse over poles – encouraging the horse to stretch.
- » As the horse becomes comfortable at this distance, shorten and lengthen the distance between the poles to encourage collection and lengthening. Try not to use the lines to make the horse shorten and lengthen. Lines may be used to support but not hold back. The horse will eventually learn to properly use muscles to shorten and lengthen on its own
- » Once walking is mastered – trot the horse changing the distance as before

EXERCISE 6 (Can be done long lining or ridden)
- » Using the whole arena (do not keep on a circle) walk 10 strides.
- » Transition to slow trot- trot 10 strides.
- » Transition back to walk – walk 10 strides.
- » Halt 5 seconds.
- » Back 5-10 strides.
- » Repeat and do numerous times in both directions.

EXERCISE 7 (Can be done long lining or ridden)
- » Set up 4 ground poles on one long side approximately 2.5 feet apart. Set up 4 ground poles raised 6" across from the others.
- » Approach ground poles and go through the center at a walk.
- » Go over several times in each direction.
- » Now do the same at the trot.

EXERCISE 8 (Ridden Exercise)
- » At a walk ride a 20-meter circle – spiral inward as small as you can while maintaining rhythm and tempo.
- » Spiral out maintaining rhythm and tempo.
- » Do the same at a trot once the walk is mastered.

EXERCISE 9 (Ridden Exercise)
» Set up ground poles end to end down the center of the arena.
» Going through the center of the poles, circle to the right on 1 & 2 when coming to #2 the second time, circle left.
» Going through the center of the poles circle to the left on 2 & 3, when coming to #3 the second time, circle right.
» Do this at a walk maintaining rhythm and tempo – when walk is mastered – try a sitting trot also maintaining rhythm and tempo. When this is mastered, alternate sitting and rising trot – do not change rhythm and tempo when rising!

EXERCISE 10 (Ridden Exercise)
» Develop a good working trot.
» Begin to shorten the reins ½" at a time until the poll is the highest point of his body – keep the trot forward and maintain this frame for 15 seconds.
» Gradually let the reins slip through your fingers ½" at a time until his poll is lower than his withers - keep the trot forward and maintain this frame for 15 seconds.
» Repeat several times and then go in the opposite direction.

EXERCISE 11 (Ridden Exercise)
» On the long side, set out 4 ground poles spaced for your horse's collected trot. About 30" beyond that set 4 more ground poles set at your horse's lengthened trot.
» Starting on the side without poles, develop a working trot.
» Before the shortened pole, collect your horse.
» Before the lengthened poles, encourage your horse to move out.
» After the lengthened poles, bring your horse back to a working trot, repeat the exercise in both directions.

EXERCISE 12 (Ridden Exercise)
» Mark out 2 - 10-meter circles side by side with poles.
» Outside the circles mark off a 20-meter circle with cones.
» Inside the box ride the 10-meter circle – sometimes changing circles by keeping straight on the sides and sometimes making a mini serpentine around the center pole.
» Occasionally leave the box and go to the 20-meter circle.
» Maintain tempo first at a walk and then a trot.

CARDIO PHASE
- » Determine your horse's fitness level
- » Take pulse and respiration at rest (under the jaw, under the tail).
- » Pulse = 32-40 beats per minute at rest (a more fit horse has a lower pulse).
- » Respiration = 12-20 breaths/minute at rest.
- » Trot horse 10-30 minutes (depending on fitness level) take pulse and respiration again.
- » Pulse normally = 75-105 after moderate work (could be 120-160 if not fit or heavy work).
- » Walk until pulse and respiration return to normal – notice how long this takes.
- » For a fit horse, pulse should return to 60 within 10-15 minutes.
- » Should return to normal within 20-30 minutes.
- » If the horse recovers to normal in 10-15 minutes, exercise may be increased.
- » Exercise the horse 3-5 times per week.
- » Make notes of the willingness and coordination improvement as the recovery time improves.
- » Positive changes will occur as quickly as 2-3 weeks.

Warm-Up is Important and will:
- » Minimize the chance of injuries
- » Increase blood flow
- » Loosen and warm up muscles and tendons
- » Supple the horse

Increasing Cardio Fitness:
- » As the fitness level improves the exercise may increase. Increase only 1 aspect at a time– intensity, distance ,or duration.
- » Interval training: 2 minutes of intense work (trotting up a hill, galloping on the flat – do something that is similar to what your end goal will be – running barrels, eventing, etc.) to bring the heart rate to 180-200 followed by a slow jog until the heart rate returns to @ 100

Cool-down is Important and will:
- » Help to remove lactic acid from the blood to minimize soreness and stiffness
- » Trot 5 minutes – walk 5 minutes – supple 5 minutes at the walk

SOURCES

UNDERSTANDING MUSIC
https://www.musicnotes.com/blog/2014/04/11/how-to-read-sheet-music/

UNDERSTANDING RHYTHM
Harris, Susan. Horsemanship in Pictures. New York: 5-H Acres School of Riding, 1972.
http://webhome.auburn.edu/~linmary/dance.html
https://www.dancing4beginners.com/rumba/
https://en.wikipedia.org/wiki/Tap_dance
https://www.royalacademyofdance.org/more/music/resources/dance-rhythms-for-ballet-pianists
Cyril William Beaumont, Enrico Cecchetti, Stanislas Idzikowski A Manual of the Theory and Practice of Classical Theatrical Dancing, London, 1922
http://www.thececchetticonnection.com/notes-from-the-author-the-journey-to-thececchetticonnection-com/

UNDERSTANDING TEMPO
https://www.usdf.org/EduDocs/Competition/GotMusicNovember2007.pdf
https://dressagetoday.com/theory/purpose-posting-trot-outside-diagonal-heather-mason
http://www.meredithmanor.edu/features/articles/drm/riding_trot.asp
https://www.hollywoodballroomdc.com/recommended-tempos-for-dance-music/
https://www.music4dance.net/dances/rumba
http://tapdancingengineer.blogspot.com/2014/02/music-theory-for-dancers-part-1-beat.html
https://www.youtube.com/watch?v=GBQtVfWsE0c

STAMINA
https://www.cnn.com/2014/05/06/sport/ballet-dressage-dancing-horse/index.html
https://www.equisearch.com/articles/exercise_better_ride_021110
https://www.active.com/fitness/calculators/heartrate
https://tone-and-tighten.com/30-minute-indoor-cardio-workout.html
https://medlineplus.gov/ency/patientinstructions/000809.htm

MUSCLE STRENGTH AND FLEXIBILITY

https://www.equisearch.com/articles/exercise_better_ride_021110
https://www.stylecraze.com/articles/types-of-aerobic-dances-and-their-benefits/
https://www.realbuzz.com/articles-interests/sports-activities/article/ballroom-dance-for-fitness/
https://woman.thenest.com/dance-aerobic-anaerobic-15312.html ballet anerobic
https://delta.dance/2018/09/training-muscles-for-ballroom-dance/ excellent
https://www.quickquickslow.com/blog/how-ballroom-and-latin-dancing-build-core-strength
http://www.humankinetics.com/excerpts/excerpts/role-of-the-core-in-dance-techniques
https://georgiadance.com/tap-whats-so-great-about-it/
https://www.thoughtco.com/benefits-of-tap-dancing-1007422
https://www.silversneakers.com/blog/fitness-tap-dancing/ muscle groups in tap dancing
https://www.reuters.com/article/us-fitness-tap-idUSTRE74F1VD20110516
https://www.womenshealthmag.com/fitness/a19928590/ballerina-core-tips/
https://www.kingofthegym.com/back-anatomy/
https://www.dancespirit.com/the_importance_of_epaulement-2326036463.html
https://www.dance-teacher.com/armed-for-tap-2392320922.html
https://www.danceplace.com/grapevine/does-your-back-hurt-after-you-dance-this-may-be-why/
https://www.verywellhealth.com/what-are-the-quadriceps-muscles-2696379
https://en.wikipedia.org/wiki/Quadriceps_femoris_muscle
http://www.rounddancing.net/dance/articles/photoessay/contracheckphoto.html

VISUALIZATION

https://www.danceinforma.com/2016/11/07/the-power-of-visualization-for-dancers/
https://www.danceadvantage.net/visualization-for-dancers/
https://www.danceextreme.com/blog/the-power-of-visualization-for-dancers/
http://thelawofattraction.org/improve-your-dancing-visualization/
https://dancesportlife.com/blog/mental-training-visualization/
https://salsabortropical.com/eye-contact-and-sense-of-touch-when-you-are-dancing/
http://www.danceaustralia.com.au/news/the-importance-of-eyeline1
https://www.dancespirit.com/do-this-not-that-how-to-be-the-master-of-eye-contact-2473329173.html
https://hubpages.com/entertainment/Where-to-Look-While-Partner-Dancing-The-Importance-of-Eye-Contact

INTENTION

https://tangotopics.com/intention-based-dancing/
https://byregion.byregion.net/articles-healers/Attention_Intention.html
http://bellaballroom.com/avoiding-awkwardness-in-dancing/
http://sflovestango.com/dancing-with-intention/
https://en.wikipedia.org/wiki/Choreography
http://terp.umd.edu/new-study-unravels-how-dancers-think-when-they-dance/
"Enlightenment Dance, Dancing your way to Eternal Bliss" by Rosane Gibson "Hozuhni"

PARTNERSHIP

https://www.dancemagazine.com/great-partnerships-2306890559.html
https://www.dancecompreview.com/10-essentials-for-successful-ballroom-dance-partnership/
https://www.entrepreneur.com/article/247971

GENERAL INFO

https://dressagetoday.com/instruction/dressage-in-terms-of-dance-30472
https://www.equisearch.com/articles/exercise_better_ride_021110
https://www.equisearch.com/discoverhorses/exercises-teach-your-body-new-patterns-improve-your-riding-html
http://blog.ed.ted.com/2018/04/02/why-dance-is-just-as-important-as-math-in-school/?fbclid=IwAR2NwZ31Idhcz5CJSDowaIDtIyTkPFHgycyNn0bvBAY9SPLJWu1KQ-wNr00
http://www.humankinetics.com/excerpts/excerpts/using-cues-and-feedback-to-learn-tap-technique

SPECIAL THANK YOU TO professional dancer Sybil Konopka Kuffa for her assitance with the "Dance your way to success" suggestions.

www.ingramcontent.com/pod-product-compliance
Lightning Source LLC
Chambersburg PA
CBHW061128070526
44584CB00033B/4252